Frequently   Asked   Interview Questions & Answers in HTML5

99% Frequently Asked Q & A

By Bandana Ojha

Introduction

HTML5 is the latest evolution of the standard that defines HTML. The term represents two different concepts. It is a new version of the language HTML, with new elements, attributes, and behaviors, and a larger set of technologies that allows the building of more diverse and powerful Web sites and applications. This book contains more than 100 frequently asked interview questions with short and straight forward answers. Rather than going through comprehensive, textbook-sized reference guides, this book includes only the information required to start his/her career as a web developer. Answers of all the questions are short and to the point. We assure that you will get here the 90% frequently asked interview questions and answers. It will help both freshers as well as experienced web developers.

1. What is HTML5?

HTML5 is the latest evolution of the standard that defines HTML. The term represents two different concepts. It is a new version of the language HTML, with new elements, attributes, and behaviors, and a larger set of technologies that allows the building of more diverse and powerful Web sites and applications.

2. What Is the difference between HTML and HTML5?

HTML has seen many updates over time, and currently, the newest HTML version is HTML5. HTML5 is of course still primarily a markup language, but it has added a plethora of features to the original HTML and has eradicated some of the strictness that was present in XHTML. The main difference between HTML and HTML5 can be that neither audio nor video is a constituent of HTML whereas both can be considered integral parts of HTML5.

3.Explain some advantages of HTML5?

Some advantages of HTML5.are:

It provides both Audio and Video support

It provides geolocation support

HTML5 is the most mobile-ready tool for developing mobile sites and apps.

It usually requires less maintenance support

It also provides more reliable storage options functionality

It helps developers to use fancier forms

4. Explain some disadvantages of HTML5?

Some disadvantages of HTML5 are:

It only provides the modern browser support

It has media licensing issues

It has a fragmentation problem.

HTML5 feature may be properly implemented in Firefox but it may create problems while implementing the same in internet explorer.

5. Name some new features of HTML5.

HTML5 introduces several new elements and attributes that helps in building a modern website.

Following are great features introduced in HTML5:

New Semantic Elements – These are like <header>, <footer>, and <section>.

Forms 2.0 – Improvements to HTML web forms where new attributes have been introduced for <input> tag.

Persistent Local Storage – To achieve without resorting to third-party plugins.

WebSocket – A next-generation bidirectional communication technology for web applications.

Server-Sent Events – HTML5 introduces events which flow from web server to the web browsers and they are called Server-Sent Events (SSE).

Canvas – This supports a two-dimensional drawing surface that you can program with JavaScript.

Audio & Video – You can embed audio or video on your web pages without resorting to third-party plugins.

Geolocation – Now visitors can choose to share their physical location with your web application.

Microdata − This lets you create your own vocabularies beyond HTML5 and extend your web pages with custom semantics.

Drag and drop − Drag and drop the items from one location to another location on the same webpage.

6. What is HTML5 Web Storage?

With web storage, web applications can store data locally within the user's browser. Before HTML5, application data had to be stored in cookies, included in every server request. Web storage is more secure, and large amounts of data can be stored locally, without affecting website performance. Unlike cookies, the storage limit is far larger (at least 5MB) and information is never transferred to the server.

7. What are the advantages of HTML5 Web Storage?

It can store 5 to 10 MB data. That is far more than what cookies have.

Web storage data is never transferred with HTTP request, so it increases the performance of the application.

Provides more space than what cookies offer so increasingly complex information can be kept.

8. What are the disadvantages of HTML5 Web Storage?

Data is stored as a simple string; manipulation is needed to store objects of different types such as Booleans, Objects, Ints and Floats.

Storage can be slow with the complex sets of data.

It can be disabled by the user or systems administrator.

9. Name some HTML5 Web Storage methods?

Below are some methods of HTML5 Web storage:

setItem(key,value): Adds a key/value pair to the sessionStorage object.

getItem(key): Retrieves the value for a given key.

clear(): Removes all key/value pairs for the sessionStorage object.

removeItem(key): Removes a key/value pair from the sessionStorage object.

key(n): Retrieves the value for a key.

10.Name types of Web Storage in HTML5?

There are two types of web storage in HTML5:

Session Storage:

It stores data of current session only. It means that the data stored in session storage clear automatically when the browser is closed.

Local Storage:

Local storage is another type of HTML5 Web Storage. In local storage, data is not deleted automatically when the current browser window is closed.

11. How to create and access a session storage object?

We can create and access a session storage as below,

Here we created "name" as session:

<script type="text/javascript">

sessionStorage.name="SSO";

document.write(sessionStorage.name);

</script>

12. What are HTML5 Graphics?

In HTML5, there are two types of graphics:

Scalable Vector Graphics (SVG)

SVG provides a big benefit, now people are using high-resolution devices (iPads and Monitors) and it becomes impressive as designs, logos and charts can scale accordingly. The HTML tag <svg> is a container for SVG graphics. SVG is used for drawing paths, circle, boxes, text and graphic images.

Canvas

A canvas is a rectangular area on HTML page for drawing graphics on the fly via JavaScript. The default size of the canvas is 300 px × 150 px (width × height). The HTML tag <canvas> is a container for Canvas graphics.

13. Name two semantic tags included in HTML5?

The <article> and <section> tags are two new tags that are included in HTML5. Articles can be composed of multiple sections that can have multiple articles. An article tag represents a full block of content which is a section of a bigger whole.

14. Which JavaScript objects are not accessible to web worker?

Following JavaScript objects are not accessible to web worker:

1. The window object

2. The document object

3. The parent object

15. What is SVG?

SVG is the abbreviation for Scalable Vector Graphics. It is used to define vector-based graphics for the Web. The graphics are defined in XML format. An important quality of SVG graphics is that their quality is maintained even when they are zoomed or resized. All the element and attributes of SVG files can be animated.

16.What are the advantages of SVG over other image format like JPEG or GIF?

Following are the main advantages of using SVG over other image formats:

- It is possible to scale the SVG images.

- They can be created and edited with any text editor.

- The print quality of these image is high at any resolution.

- It is possible to zoom the SVG images without any degradation in the quality.

- SVG images can be searched, indexed, scripted, and compressed.

17.Differentiate between Canvas and SVG?

Some important differences between Canvas and SVG are:

1. Canvas is resolution dependent whereas SVG is resolution independent.
2. In case of SVG, an event handler can be associated with the drawing object whereas Canvas doesn't support event handlers to be associated with the drawing objects.
3. SVG is slower than Canvas as in the case of SVG, co-ordinates need to be remembered for later manipulation purpose
4. Canvas is suitable for graphics intensive gaming purpose whereas SVG is not suitable for gaming

18.What is a Canvas? What is the default border size of a canvas?

- Canvas is a rectangular area on a HTML page, specified with the tag <canvas>.

- By default, a canvas has no border. To get a border on the canvas, a style attribute is required to be used.

19.Which methods are used to draw a straight line on a Canvas?

Following methods are used to draw a straight line on a Canvas:

1. moveTo(x,y) – It defines the starting co-ordinates of the line.

2. lineTo(x,y) – It defines the ending co-ordinates of the line.

3. The actual line is drawn with the help of a method like stroke()

20.What are gradients in Canvas used for? What are their different types?

Gradients in canvas are used to fill rectangles, circles, lines etc.

The gradients in Canvas are of two types:

1. createLinearGradient(x,y,x1,y1) – It creates a linear gradient

2. createRadialGradient(x,y,r,x1,y1,r1) – It creates a radial/circular gradient

Which method is used to draw an image on the canvas?

drawImage(image,x,y) method is used to draw an image on the canvas.

21. Give an example of adding canvas in Html5?

```
<canvas id="myCanvas" width="200" height="100"></canvas>
```

22. Which browsers support HTML5?

The latest versions of Google Chrome, Apple Safari, Mozilla Firefox, and Opera all support most of the HTML5 features.

23. Is HTML5 backward compatible with old browsers?

Yes! HTML5 is designed, as much as possible, to be backward compatible with existing web browsers. New features build on existing features and allow you to provide fallback content for older browsers.

It is suggested to detect support for individual HTML5 features using a few lines of JavaScript.

24 What is <figure> in HTML5?

This tag represents a piece of self-contained flow content. It is mostly used as a single unit as a reference the main flow of the document.

25. What are the new media elements in Html5?

Below are the New Media Elements have added in HTML5

<audio> For multimedia content, sounds, music or other audio streams.

<video> For video content, such as a movie clip or other video streams.

<source> For media resources for media elements, defined inside video or audio.

elements.

<embed> For embedded content, such as a plug-in.

<track> For text tracks used in media players.

26. Is canvas element used in Html5?

Yes, we can use Canvas element in html5 like below
<canvas>.

27. What are the new Form elements made available in HTML5?

The new Form elements in HTML5 provide for a better functionality. The tags provided to carry out these functions are:

1) <datalist> - It specifies a list of options for input controls. These options are pre-defined.

2) <keygen> - This tag defines a key-pair generator field.

3) <output> - It defines the result of a calculation.

28. What is audio tag in HTML 5?

This new element allows you to deliver audio files directly through the browser, without the need for any plug-ins. The Audio tag is a new tag introduced in HTML5. You can use it to play audio sound like .mp3, wav, and .ogg. I have used five types of sound formats to show which formats are compatible for the browsers. A WAV file is a common sound format that is supported by most browser versions.

Syntax

<audio src="URL" controls> </audio>

29.What are the rules established for HTML5?

Some rules for HTML5 were established:

New features should be based on HTML, CSS, DOM, and JavaScript

Reduce the need for external plugins (like Flash)

Better error handling

More markup to replace scripting

HTML5 should be device independent

The development process should be visible to the public.

30. What are Web Workers APIs in HTML 5?

Web Workers APIs provide a way in JavaScript to run something in the background that can-do tasks without interfering with the user interface. As per the W3C standard "It is a JavaScript script executed from an HTML page that runs in the background, independently of other user-interface scripts that may also have been executed from the same HTML page. Web workers are able to utilize multi-core CPUs more effectively."

31. What are the different types of web workers?

Types of web workers:

      Dedicated workers

      Shared workers

32. What is the difference between dedicated worker and shared worker?

Dedicated web worker:

A dedicated worker is accessible from the parent script that created it

It is simply tied to its main connection

It has a wide browser support

Shared worker:

A shared worker can be accessed from any script of the same origin

It can work with multiple connections

Limited browser support: Chrome 4.0+, Safari 5.0+ and Opera 10.6+

33. How do web workers work?

Web Workers work in the following three steps:

First it should be executed on separate threads.

It should be hosted in separate files from the main page.

Finally, a Worker object needs to be instantiated to call them.

34. What is the application cache in HTML5?

The Application Cache concept means that a web application is cached. It can be accessible without the need for internet connection.

35. Why Application Cache is used?

Some advantages of Application Cache:

1.   Offline browsing – Web users can also use the application when they are offline.

2.   Speed – Cached resources load quicker

3.   Reduce the server load – The web browser will only download updated resources from the server.

36. What is WebSQL?

WebSQL is a structured relational database at the client browser side. It's a local RDBMS inside the browser on which you can fire SQL queries.

37. Is WebSQL a part of HTML 5 specification?

No, many people label it as HTML 5 but it's not part of HTML 5 specification. The specification is based around SQLite.

38. What are the deprecated elements in HTML5 from HTML4?

Elements that are deprecated from HTML 4 to HTML 5 are:

frame

frameset

noframe

applet

big

center

basefront

39. What is cache manifest file in HTML5?

Cache manifest file is simply a text file that dictates the browser, what to store for offline access. It lists down the required resources for offline access.

40. Explain different section of a manifest file?

There are three sections of a manifest file:

1) cache manifest - Files listed here are cached after they are downloaded for the first time.

2) network - Files listed here require a connection to the server and are never cached.

3) fallback - Files listed here specify fallback pages if a page is inaccessible.

41.What is the difference between HTML5 application cache and regular HTMl browser cache?

One of the key features of HTML 5 is *Application Cache* that enables us to make an offline version of a web application. It allows to fetch few or all of website contents such as HTML files, CSS, images, java script, etc. locally. This feature speeds up the site performance. This is achieved with the help of a manifest file defined as follows:

<!doctype html>

42. Can HTML5 get the geographical position of a user?

- Yes, HTML5 can get the location of a user with the use of Geolocation API.

- Use getCurrentPosition() method to get the user's current position.

43 What is a hyperlink?

A hyperlink is a text/image on a webpage, which when clicked redirects to a new web page.

44. What is an API in HTML5?

API stands for Application Programming Interfaces and is a way to create applications. They use pre-built components. Using the available APIs, developers can integrate the features into their websites.

45. What are the drawbacks of cookies?

Cookies have following drawbacks–

Cookies are included with every HTTP request, thereby slowing down your web application by transmitting the same data.

Cookies are included with every HTTP request, thereby sending data unencrypted over the internet.

Cookies are limited to about 4 KB of data. Not enough to store required data.

46. What are web sockets?

Web Sockets is a next-generation bidirectional communication technology for web applications which operates over a single socket and is exposed via a JavaScript interface in HTML 5 compliant browsers.

Once you get a Web Socket connection with the web server, you can send data from browser to server by calling a send() method and receive data from server to browser by an on-message event handler.

47.How to create a web socket object?

Following is the API which creates a new WebSocket object.

var Socket = new WebSocket (URL, [protocal]);

Here first argument, URL, specifies the URL to which to connect. The second attribute, protocol is optional, and if present, specifies a sub-protocol that the server must support for the connection to be successful.

48.What is the purpose of Socket.readyState atribute of WebSocket?

The readonly attribute readyState represents the state of the connection. It can have the following values:

A value of 0 indicates that the connection has not yet been established.

A value of 1 indicates that the connection is established, and communication is possible.

A value of 2 indicates that the connection is going through the closing handshake.

A value of 3 indicates that the connection has been closed or could not be opened.

49.What is the purpose of Socket.bufferedAmount atribute of WebSocket?

The readonly attribute bufferedAmount represents the number of bytes of UTF-8 text that have been queued using send() method.

50. What is the use of Fieldset tag in HTML5?

The <fieldset> tag groups related form elements. It is like a box. In other words, it draws a box around related element.

It must start with a <legend>tag because the <legend> tag defines the title of the field set.

By using the <fieldset>tag and the <legend> tag, you can make your form much easier to understand for the users.

51. Describe Progress Bar in HTML 5?

Sometimes a task is running within a program that might take a while to complete. A user-friendly program provides some information to the user that the task is happening. It also tells how long the task might take and how much the task has been done or completed. One of the best ways to show all these activities is with the Progress Bar control. In a simple way, the progress bar indicates the progress of a specific task.

In HTML 5, there is the element "progress" that displays the progress of a task.

Syntax:

<progress></progress>

52. What Is The < !doctype > ? Is it necessary to use in Html5?

The <!DOCTYPE> is an instruction to the web browser about what version of HTML the page is written in. AND The <!DOCTYPE> tag does not have an end tag and It is not case sensitive.

The <!DOCTYPE> declaration must be the very first thing in HTML5 document, before the <html> tag. As In HTML 4.01, all <! DOCTYPE > declarations require a reference to a Document Type Definition (DTD), because HTML 4.01 was based on Standard Generalized Markup Language (SGML). WHERE AS HTML5 is not based on SGML, and therefore does not require a reference to a Document Type Definition (DTD).

53. What are the different kinds of Doctypes available?

The three kinds of Doctypes which are available:

Strict Doctype

Transitional Doctype

Frameset Doctype

54.What is the browser cache?

Caching is the concept of intelligently storing commonly used data in quick-to-access locations so that requesting that data will happen as fast as possible. The browser cache is a small database of files that contains downloaded web page resources, such as images, videos, CSS, Java script, and so on.

55. How does the browser know what to cache?

As defined in the HTTP spec, each request and response can have headers associated with it, and it's through these headers that the server can tell the client what to cache and for how long. There are two modern HTTP response headers that define how a resource should be cached: Cache-Control and ETag.

56. What is span tag?

The HTML <span> tag is used for grouping and applying styles to inline elements. It is mostly used for styling by using an id or class.

57.What is the difference between span tag and div tag?

The difference between span and div is that a span tag is in-line and usually used for a small chunk of HTML inside a line (such as inside a paragraph) whereas a div (division) element is block-line (which is basically equivalent to having a line-break before and after it) and used to group larger chunks of code.

58. Does span need a closing tag?

Span tag is a paired tag, that means it has both open (<) and closing (>) tag and it is mandatory to close the tag.

59. What is meta tag?

A meta tag is a tag in HTML that describes some aspect of the contents of a Web page. The information that you provide in a meta tag is used by search engines to index a page so that someone searching for the kind of information the page contains will be able to find it. The meta tag is placed near the top of the HTML in a Web page as part of the heading.

60. What is the function of a meta tag?

Meta elements are typically used to specify page description, keywords, author of the document, last modified, and other metadata. The metadata can be used by browsers (how to display content or reload page), search engines (keywords), or other web services.

61. What is meter tag?

The <meter> tag defines a scalar measurement within a known range, or a fractional value. This is also known as a gauge.

62. What is the difference between progress and meter tag?

The progress tag is used to represent the progress of the task while the meter tag is used to measure data within a given range.

63. Explain Microdata in HTML5.

Using Microdata, the metadata is nested within existing content on web pages. Search engines extract the microdata from a web page to provide a good browsing experience.

64. What is the best way to group form elements?

The <fieldset> tag can be used to group some of the form elements. When the purpose is to provide some HTML elements as a group to the user then, fieldset tag is the best one to use. It takes another tag in it <legend> which provides a title to the grouped elements.

65. What is the use of the article element in HTML5?

Article is a HTML5 semantic element, similar to <section> and <header> . It is most commonly used to contain information that may be distributed independently from the rest of the site or application it appears in.

66. What is the use of aside tag in html5?

The aside element represents a section of a page that consists of content that is tangentially related to the content around the aside element, and which could be considered separate from that content. Such sections are often represented as sidebars in printed typography.

67. What is Geolocation API in HTML?

HTML5 Geolocation API lets you share your location with your favorite web sites. A JavaScript can capture your latitude and longitude and can be sent to backend web server and do fancy location-aware things like finding local businesses or showing your location on a map.

68. What is purpose of getCurrentPosition() method of geolocation object of HTML5?

This method retrieves the current geographic location of the user.

69. What is purpose of watchPosition() method of geolocation object of HTML5?

This method retrieves periodic updates about the current geographic location of the device.

70.What is purpose of clearPosition() method of geolocation object of HTML5?

This method cancels an ongoing watchPosition call.

71. What is Contenteditable in html5?

The contenteditable attribute specifies whether the content of an element is editable or not.When the contenteditable attribute is not set on an element, the element will inherit it from its parent.

72. What is the role of the WBR element in html5?

The <wbr> (Word Break Opportunity) tag specifies where in a text it would be ok to add a line-break. Tip: When a word is too long, or you are afraid that the browser will break your lines at the wrong place, you can use the <wbr> element to add word break opportunities.

73. Can an HTML element have multiple classes?

Specifies one or more class names for an element. To specify multiple classes, separate the class names with a space, e.g. <span class="left important">. This allows you to combine several CSS classes for one HTML element.

74. What is Onblur and Onfocus HTML?

The onblur event occurs when an object loses focus. The onblur event is most often used with form validation code (e.g. when the user leaves a form field). Tip: The onblur event is the opposite of the onfocus event.

75. What is Server-Side Events in HTML5?

Along with HTML5, WHATWG Web Applications 1.0 introduces events which flow from web server to the web browsers and they are called Server-Sent Events (SSE). Using SSE, you can push DOM events continuously from your web server to the visitor's browser. The event streaming approach opens a persistent connection to the server, sending data to the client when new information is available, eliminating the need for continuous polling. Server-sent events standardizes how we stream data from the server to the client.

76. What is Flexbox in HTML 5?

Flexbox is not a single property but a set of properties on the parent element and their children. Basically, the parent is a container. It is probably a div called a flex container and the children are the elements called flex items.

77.What are the attributes of Flexbox?

Following are the attributes of the flex box.

Main axis: The main axis is the default flow direction for the flex items.

Main-start and Main-end: The main-start and main-end are the starting point and ending point for the flex items to flow in the flex container.

Cross axis: The cross axis is perpendicular to the main axis.

Cross-start and Cross-end: The flex items are placed from the start at the cross-start point and ends at cross-end point.

Main size: The flex items width or height in the main dimension is the main size of the flexbox.

Cross size: The flex items width or height in the cross dimension is the cross size of the flexbox.

78. What are Frames in HTML?

Frames allow multiple HTML documents to be present as independent windows within a main browser. They allow you to present two or more documents at once.

79. Name different types of Frames?

There are two types of frames based on their layout.

1.   Vertical Frames

2.   Horizontal Frames

80. Describe MathML in HTML5?

The Mathematical Markup Language (MathML) is a markup language to show mathematical and scientific content on the Web. HTML5 allows us to use MathML elements inside a document using $...$ tags. A mathematical expression must be inserted into the element <math> with a specified namespace.

81. What happens if the list-style-type property is used on a non-list element like a paragraph?

If the list-style-type property is used on a non-list element like a paragraph, the property will be ignored and do not affect the paragraph.

82. Explain the usage of HTML5 semantic elements?

The usage of the different HTML5 semantic elements are described below:

<header>: It is mainly used to store and define the starting information about a web page section.

<article>: It is used to define a set of information which can be logically independent and can be described with respect to the concerned web page business logic.

<section>: It mainly consists of a set of instructions that defines the basic structure and content of the page

<footer>: This is used to hold a set of information that is getting displayed at the last portion of a webpage

83. Name the audio formats supported in Html5?

Ogg Vorbis, MP3, WAV are the audio formats supported in Html5.

84. What is web forms 2.0 in Html5?

Forms Section in HTML5 is known as Web Forms 2.0. It's basically an extension to HTML4 forms features. Web Forms 2.0 in HTML5 provides comparatively a greater degree of semantic markups than HTML4 as well as removing the need of lengthy and tedious scripting and styling, as a result making HTML5 richer but simpler in use.

85. What are the most commonly used List tags?

The list tags are used to list out any information.

There are three list types in HTML:

unordered list — used to group a set of related items in no specific order

ordered list — used to group a set of related items in a specific order

description list — used to display name/value pairs such as terms and definitions

86. What CORS in HTML5?

Cross-origin resource sharing (CORS) is a mechanism used to allow limited resources from another domain in a web browser

For example, when the user clicks on HTML5- video player, it asks for camera permission and if the user allows permission then only camera will be opened, else it will not open the camera for web applications.

87. How do you play a Video using HTML5?

HTML5 defines a new element to embed a video on Web Page

the <video> element.

Example:

<video width="500" height="300" controls>

<source src= "video1.mp4" type= "video/mp4">

</video>

88.How do you play an Audio using HTML5?

HTML5 defines a new element to embed a video on Web Page

the <audio> element.

Example:

<audio controls>

<source src= "audio.mp3" type= "audio/mpeg" >

</audio>

89. Why form tag is used in HTML?

The HTML <form> tag is used for creating a form for user input. A form can contain textfields, checkboxes, radio-buttons and more. Forms are used to pass user-data to a specified URL.

90. How to create a form tag in HTML?

The <form> tag in HTML is used to create form for user input. There are many elements which are used within form tag. For example: <input>, <textarea>, <button>, <select>, <option>, <optgroup>, <fieldset>, <label>.

91. What is the use of action in form tag?

The action attribute is used to inform the browser what page (or script) to call when the "submit" button is pressed.

92. What is Novalidate attribute in form tag?

The novalidate attribute is a Boolean attribute, when present, it specifies that the form-data (input) should not be validated when submitted.

93. What is keygen in HTML5?

The <keygen> element generates an encryption key for passing encrypted data to a server. When an HTML form is submitted, the browser will generate a key pair and store the private key in the browser's local key storage and send the public key to the server.

94. What is Datalist in html5?

The <datalist> tag specifies a list of pre-defined options for an <input> element. The <datalist> tag is used to provide an "autocomplete" feature on <input> elements.

95. Which method checks if the browser can play the specified video type?

The canPlayType() method checks if the browser can play the specified audio/video type. The canPlayType() method can return one of the following values: "probably" - the browser most likely supports this audio/video type. "maybe" - the browser might support this audio/video type.

96. Which html5 tag would you use to define footer?

HTML5 <footer> Element. The <footer> element specifies a footer for a document or section. A <footer> element should contain information about its containing element. A footer typically contains the author of the document, copyright information, links to terms of use, contact information, etc.

97. What is action and method in form?

The method attribute specifies how to send form-data (the form-data is sent to the page specified in the action attribute). The form-data can be sent as URL variables (with method="get") or as HTTP post transaction (with method="post").

98. What is the usage of the cite tag?

The cite tag is used to represent the title of a work (like a book, paper, poem etc). This tag is mostly used as an inline tag.

99. What is WHATWG?

The Web Hypertext Application Technology Working Group (WHATWG) is a community of people interested in evolving the web through standards and tests.

The WHATWG was founded by individuals of Apple, the Mozilla Foundation, and Opera Software in 2004, after a W3C workshop. Apple, Mozilla and Opera were becoming increasingly concerned about the W3C's direction with XHTML, lack of interest in HTML, and apparent disregard for the needs of real-world web developers. So, in response, these organizations set out with a mission to address these concerns and the Web Hypertext Application Technology Working Group was born.

100. What is Modernizr?

Modernizr is a small piece of JavaScript code that automatically detects the availability of next-generation web technologies in your user's browsers. Rather than blacklisting entire ranges of browsers based on "UA sniffing," Modernizr uses feature detection to allow you to easily tailor your user's experiences based on the actual capabilities of their browser.

101.Why Modernizr is needed?

All web developers come up against differences between browsers and devices. That's largely due to different feature sets: the latest versions of the popular browsers can do some awesome things which older browsers can't – but we still must support the older ones.

Modernizr makes it easy to deliver tiered experiences: make use of the latest and greatest features in browsers which support them, without leaving less fortunate users high and dry.

102. When a local storage data gets deleted?

Local storage data has no time limit. To clear a local storage setting you would need to call localStorage.remove('key'); where 'key' is the key of the value you want to remove. If you want to clear all settings, you need to call localStorage.clear() method.

103. Can you use MathML tags directly in HTML5 without any plugin?

Yes! The HTML syntax of HTML5 allows for MathML elements to be used inside a document using $...$ tags.

105. What is Web messaging?

Web Messaging is the way for documents to separates browsing context to share the data without Dom. It overrides the cross-domain communication problem in different domains, protocols or ports.

106. What is Message Event?

Message events fires Cross-document messaging, channel messaging, server-sent events and web sockets.it has described by Message Event interface.

107. How to send a cross-document message?

Before sending a cross document message, we need to create a new web browsing context either by creating new iframe or new window. We can send the data using with postMessage() and it has two arguments.

message – The message to send

targetOrigin – Origin name

Our other best-selling books are-

100+ Frequently Asked Interview Q & A in Robotic Process Automation (RPA)

500+ Java & J2EE Interview Questions & Answers-Java & J2EE Programming

200+ Frequently Asked Interview Questions & Answers in iOS Development

200 + Frequently Asked Interview Q & A in SQL, PL/SQL, Database Development & Administration

200+ Frequently Asked Interview Questions & Answers in Manual Testing

200+ Frequently Asked Interview Q & A in Python Programming

100+ Frequently Asked Interview Questions & Answers in Robotic Process Automation- RPA

100+ Frequently Asked Interview Q & A in Cyber Security

100+ Frequently Asked Interview Questions & Answers in Scala

100+ Frequently Asked Interview Q & A in Swift Programming

100+ Frequently Asked Interview Questions & Answers in Android Development

Frequently asked Interview Q & A in Java programming

Frequently Asked Interview Questions & Answers in J2EE

Frequently asked Interview Q & A in Angular JS

Frequently asked Interview Q & A in Database Testing

Frequently asked Interview Q & A in Mobile Testing

Frequently asked Interview Q & A in Test Automation-Selenium Testing

Frequently asked Interview Questions & Answers in JavaScript

www.ingramcontent.com/pod-product-compliance
Lightning Source LLC
Chambersburg PA
CBHW031250050326
40690CB00007B/1032